The Necessary

Poetics of

Atheism

Also by Martín Espada
Vivas to Those Who Have Failed
The Meaning of the Shovel
The Trouble Ball
Soldados en el Jardín
La Tumba de Buenaventura Roig
Crucifixion in the Plaza de Armas
The Republic of Poetry
Alabanza: New & Selected Poems
A Mayan Astronomer in Hell's Kitchen
Imagine the Angels of Bread
City of Coughing and Dead Radiators
Rebellion is the Circle of a Lover's Hands
Trumpets from the Islands of Their Eviction
The Immigrant Iceboy's Bolero
His Hands Were Gentle: Selected Lyrics of Víctor Jara (*editor*)

Also by Lauren Marie Schmidt
Two Black Eyes and a Patch of Hair Missing
Psalms of The Dining Room

Also by J. D. Schraffenberger
The Waxen Poor
Saint Joe's Passion
Manifold Nature:
John Burroughs and the North American Review (*editor*)
The Great Sympathetic:
Walt Whitman and the North American Review (*editor*)

The Necessary

Poetics of

Atheism

Essays and Poems

Martín Espada

Lauren Marie Schmidt

J. D. Schraffenberger

Foreword by Andrew Sneddon
Introduction by Heid E. Erdrich

Twelve Winters Press

The Necessary Poetics of Atheism: Essays and Poems was first published by Twelve Winters Press in 2016. Some of the poems have been published elsewhere and appear here by permission of their authors.

P. O. Box 414, Sherman, Illinois 62684-0414

Visit at twelvewinters.com; email xii.winters@gmail.com; follow @twelvewinters on Twitter; and twelvewinterspress on Facebook.

Cover and interior page design by TWP Design.

Cover art copyright © 2015 Jeff Williams. *Green Division*. Used by permission. All rights reserved. Visit www.jeffveloart.com.

Author photos used by permission. All rights reserved.

ISBN
978-0-9861597-3-2
Printed in the United States of America

Publisher's Note

In June 2015, my wife Melissa and I attended the *North American Review* Bicentennial Conference in Cedar Falls, Iowa. One presentation in particular was a big draw, and conferees packed into a large and nicely appointed room to hear "The Necessary Poetics of Atheism," by Martín Espada, Lauren Schmidt and Jeremy Schraffenberger. Their individual papers, which included readings of their poems, and the discussion that followed were so electrifying that the conference's schedule was actually thrown off-kilter as those in attendance didn't want to leave. Jeremy, who also served as the conference director, was forced to bring the session to a close and get everyone moving again.

Twelve Winters Press brought out Jeremy (J. D.) Schraffenberger's second collection of poems, *The Waxen Poor* (a book which was named a Best Book of 2015 by *Chicago Book Review*); and that evening, still feeling the energy of the atheism panel, it came to me that the Press should turn the presentation into a book. Clearly the topic, especially as it was contextualized by the three poets, struck a chord that resonated with the dozens of people who attended their panel. I had trouble sleeping I was so excited about the possibility. Finally at around five a.m. I texted the idea to Jeremy, and later that day (day two of the conference) he was able to confirm that Martín and Lauren were interested in the project too.

It has taken more than a year to pull everything together, including a foreword by Andrew Sneddon, an introduction by Heid E. Erdrich, and cover art generously made available by Jeff Williams, but in all that time my excitement for the project has not waned at all. So it is with great pleasure that Twelve Winters Press makes available to the world *The Necessary Poetics of Atheism: Essays and Poems*.

Ted Morrissey
Sherman, Illinois

Contents

FOREWORD

ATHEISTS THINK that it is not the case that gods exist. Such disbelief is all that many people associate with atheism. Since this idea is all that necessarily unites atheists, this common association is understandable. It is not accurate, however. "God" is the linchpin in a vast, messy network of ideas. These other ideas are as common as that of "god." What is less common is to recognize their essentially religious nature, including their relation to the idea of "god."

We live with shared ways of thinking and acting that are shot through with religious assumptions. One of the things that sometimes happens when people become convinced that there are no gods is that their consciousness about other religious presuppositions is raised. This can be a burden. When you give up on the notion of "god," it can be tiresome to bump into much the same idea in other forms. "God Bless You" as a greeting streaks our casual meetings with freighted undertones. "Merry Christmas" loses its convivial simplicity. These are relatively trivial cases. Much more subtle are the myriad concepts that only make sense in a religious framework but that show up without overtly religious marks. "Soul," "spirit," "gift," and many others await the atheist around every corner.

This language is not inert. It deeply shapes the ways in which we think. Many habits of thought and action are essentially yet covertly religious. Seeing the hand of god in natural beauty is such a habit. Claiming that everything happens for a reason is another one. To become an atheist is to have a growing awareness of these linguistic and behavioral burdens and to face considerable work rooting them out of one's life.

At the same time, the network of "god" concepts presents atheists with both opportunity and hope. Insofar as we wish for others to give up these bankrupt ideas, the many complex links found here present many inroads to disbelief. One person enters via distrust of the idea of the supernatural. Another gives up god through reasoning about moral considerations. Another person is impressed by the naturalistic achievements of centuries of scientific explanation, and so on. We can hope for growing ranks of the godfree on many fronts.

If we wish to help people to become atheists, to change the habits of talk and thought that constitute our shared intellectual space, well, the religious tapestry presents many threads on which to pull. Some people do their part through living publicly godfree and good lives. Others contribute to the delivery of an accurate view of the nature of the world, including ourselves, with which to replace religious ones. Still others work via the classic philosophical task of making and criticizing arguments.

This brings me to beauty, both natural and, especially, artificial. Much of art is explicitly religious, and much deploys essentially religious concepts without being about religion, exactly. But very little is explicitly godfree. This is an opportunity. One of the ways to live in public, to work and to show others what atheism can be like, is through art.

Consider seeing art through godfree eyes. I am a North American, but I like to vacation in Europe. Like many tourists I regularly visit European churches. I'm there not for the gods but for the art. The Alhambra, St. Peter's, Sagrada Familia—fantastic! It's the same with galleries. Christian, Roman, and Greeks gods, Muslim gardens and tile patterns—I wish I were there now! The religious messages are diverse but clear: humans are broken, god is perfect, and by extension the eternal is to be sought by all (but feared by the wicked!).

To just what aspects of beauty does atheism attune us? In the case of buildings and paintings, the religious interpretation leads our eye away from the surfaces of bodies and towards the supernatural beyond. The godfree eye can dwell on the bodies themselves. Humans aren't necessarily broken, but we are fragile. The tortured bodies and myriad tears found in religious art are an ironic testament to our contingent well-being. On this platform the exaggerated hopes and fears of religion make sense. Life can be awful: the good moments rarely last, while the bad ones are inevitable. Some of this is due to chance, but some is due to malice of other people. Why not hope for eternal well-being? Why not hope that the bastards get their due? The atheist can see this as the forlorn desperation of thoughtful apes.

Some people find this sort of thing very easy to do. For instance, when I mentioned to my neighbor that I was going to visit Spain, she noted being struck by the bloodiness of the Christian imagery she saw in paintings there. I don't know whether my neighbor is an atheist or not; seeing, noting and remembering the blood years later came naturally to her. Others will find this difficult. Atheist consciousness-raising can take deliberate retraining of one's sensibility, by oneself and with the aid and direction of others. When I got to Spain I looked for the blood!

Where religions tend to emphasize eternity, an atheist's sensibility is tuned to temporality. The recurring tile patterns of Moorish art show us the ideas of a particular historically situated people frozen in time. The varied faces of Sagrada Família show us the changing yet linked concerns and values of several generations of Barcelonan Catholics.

The religious exaltation of eternity strikes me as particularly blind to the wonders of nature. A godfree eye is better suited to registering natural beauty. If religion has an ideal season, it's winter: everything is still, frozen as it is, an unchanging expanse of virgin snow stretching before you forever. The ideal godfree season is spring. Life sprouts and changes very quickly. As I write these words, the lilacs in my neighborhood are variously blooming and passing. The magnolias have already had their lush yet sparse blossoms spread over the ground by the season's new rain-showers. One round of dandelions has come and gone; another will follow. The temporary fragility of spring is wonderful after the long, cold winter. I am tempted by the religious urge to want to freeze spring's wonders, but I know better and I resist.

Images are one thing, words are another. Words are a particularly important focal point for art made from an atheist's perspective because of the hidden and powerful concepts that tend to form our habits of thought and talk. Our godly habits are reified in our vocabulary. Some people aim at reworking our religious concepts in a way that shears them of their religious content and suits them to atheistic ears. This is very difficult work, but the impulse is understandable. Since people already use these concepts, repurposing them gets a godfree worldview a foot in the door.

Just as much, however, an atheistic poetics needs a new vocabulary. By "new" I do not mean "from the ground up, radically new." I mean a way of speaking of the world and of what matters in it that eschews the religiously weighted vocabulary (and concerns, and metaphors, and habits, and so on), and that instead retrains the ear to attend to our fragility and temporality and the tongue to speak of truths, both hard and beautiful, instead of vain hopes and empty fears.

Poems are about lots of things. But every poem, whatever else its subject, draws our attention to its wordiness. Poems are about everything, yet always about language itself. This should not be underestimated. The religious impulse is to make too much of us. It portrays us as children of god, servants yet special, contenders for eternal bliss while threatened with eternal torture. These are empty threats and promises. Humans are neither broken angels nor the imperfect creations of a divine mind nor the only animals imbued with a divine spark. However, we are unique, and a large part of what makes us unique is language. A godfree poetics retrains our ear away from the divine and towards our words and our wordiness. We are the speaking apes; this is worth remembering, indeed cherishing.

Religion encourages thoughts about transcendence. The godly aesthetic mode is to try to go beyond the here-and-now towards the would-be eternal, to eschew the natural and imperfect for the supernatural and perfect. An aesthetic that gives up on the existence of gods has no role for a transcendent attitude towards natural and artificial beauty. Instead, let us call an atheist poetics "grounded." The grounded eye sees the surfaces of bodies in their fragile contingency. The grounded ear hears and appreciates the time-bounded achievement of our wordy efforts at explanation, celebration and sharing. The grounded tongue sings of its place in the glorious world of spring, of its hopes for better days, and of its grim recognition that nothing lasts. A grounded poetic makes no more yet no less of us than we are.

A grounded worldview would be an achievement. As I write, the worldview that we share and that is passed from one generation to another is not grounded. Far from it: it is one that hopes for yet fears the transcendent. When I'm optimistic I suspect that it will be a few generations before it is a godfree set of concepts and habits that we pass on to our offspring. When I'm pessimistic I doubt that this will ever happen. When I'm particularly gloomy I suspect that this is the best moment that we will ever have to be atheists, and it's not a particularly good one.

The poems and ruminations offered in this book offer a counterpoint to my gloom. They are a rich and diverse set of fingers pulling at the threads of the religious blanket under which it is so easy to seek false comfort. They retrain our ears to hear the concerns and hopes of the worldly mammals that we are. They take concrete steps, moving and humorous ones, to retrain our minds away from religious habits of thought and talk and towards grounded ones. Against the icy crystalline fingers of religion's winter, these poems are fleeting magnolia petals marking, I hope, the creeping dawn of an atheist spring.

Andrew Sneddon
May 30, 2016

Introduction

ONCE I HAD a friend who was an Episcopal priest. He told me about the theory of "The God Spot"—which scientists have identified as the biological mechanism of faith. I asked him if, having researched the place in the brain where faith is maintained, he could retain his belief in God. He said yes emphatically. I pushed further. I asked if he thought his faith was real or an illusion of biology. Such a distinction did not matter, he said. His biology was real and his faith was real and the two were not, as I would have thought, mutually exclusive. He also told me that there seem to be individuals who lack a biological predisposition to belief in God. I've never read up on that possibility because I found it such a relief to think atheism may be as natural as belief. I do not want to find out if lack of a God Spot is common or extremely rare. Image and anti-image sometimes make a slippery aesthetic. For instance, atheist poems can be, understandably, confusingly reverent in tone. The absence of God becomes powerful in itself, a "dark absence" in Martín Espada's work, so in one poem removing a crucifix results in a miracle.

Poets who write about atheism are, perhaps, quite rare. Being godless is, as poet and contributor to *The Necessary Poetics of Atheism* Lauren Marie Schmidt suggests, a risk. In her essay she places her own work in the context of her disbelief stating first that "Godlessness is taboo" and later "I write atheist poetry, but I understand the cost of doing so," and Schmidt goes on to show us risks to every aspect of her life in writing as an atheist, including her understanding of why she lost a job at a Catholic school.

That sense of risk and taboo is meaningful to me, too, because as an Ojibwe tribal member, I come from deeply faithful people whose spiritual beliefs and practices infuse culture, language, governance, medicine—everything. And yet, as I open my life to my inherited culture, I find, as my priest friend found, my belief or lack thereof does not matter to my engagement of Ojibwe ways. Still, it pains me that my poems, and most Native American writers' poems, are inevitably read as *spiritual*, which means to many, *religious*. The idea of an American Indian atheist is unusual at best, unthinkable at worst. Perhaps even more so than the poets contained in this book, we are barred from expressing, questioning, or investigating atheism and I can appreciate why. Freedom of American Indian religious practices was not protected in the United States until 1978, a year I remember. Our ancestors fought, died, and survived for our beliefs so who are we to deny them now? What we believe or do not believe does not matter as much as our freedom to believe.

In literature, one way to know a subject is really taboo is when no one will join the conversation and few stand up to confess. Along with the poets whose work is presented here, we have several times tried to present on atheism, but we have not found a forum. My hope is that this anthology breaks a silence and gives poets and readers a way to unlock a layer of their work for the audience I know is there.

These three essays influenced me already. Recently we watched one of my favorite guilty-pleasure films and I saw it differently because of the deeply thoughtful writings in *The Necessary Poetics of Atheism*. My son is in his late teens now and we are enjoying all the scary movies we denied him as a child. The movie we watched last is *Signs*, an M. Night Shyamalan work, starring my un-favorite actor Mel Gibson as a protestant priest who lost his faith after the accidental death of his wife. Because *The Necessary Poetics of Atheism* had mapped for me an aesthetics of atheism, the film fell flat for the first time. I noted how it played out an easy trope of faith tested (death of wife), despair (loss of faith) answered by God (signs from God encoded in dying words), and reward (spoiler: not for the aliens). Atheism in this film and in much literature, is only a temporary state, a misstep, a stage one goes through. It could not possibly be that some of us are just not biologically equipped for deep faith in a superior being, or that atheism can be a thoughtfully motivated choice or inherent stance made for the betterment of humanity—which is exactly how we see it in the diverse and profoundly engaging poems presented and contextualized in *The Necessary Poetics of Atheism*.

Watching *Signs* this time also made me alert to how infrequently an atheistic worldview is presented in a positive light in popular culture and how little guidance atheists have in recovering from the faith they were born to as they are leading life, raising kids, dealing with their extreme minority status globally and so on. In *Signs*, Gibson's character (the ex-priest whose kids clearly believe in God) lives on a farm where crop circles appear and are quickly followed by terrifying aliens. Aliens horrified my son more than any other monster when he was small. He detested imagery of goopy aliens in cartoons and would physically shudder when mentioning them. Sometimes, thinking of aliens, he could not fall asleep. At those times, we did not coo to him *there's no such thing as aliens*. We told him that there's no proof aliens exist. That did not much calm him.

Atheism is not much calming. And yet it can be. In my son's fear I almost saw it happen, the old trope in action, the offering of faith in God to make a child feel safe—but those moments did not sway me from my convictions. That sounds almost like faith, I know. One of the most curious aspects of these poems on atheism is that they are full of references to God and religion, to moments of tested morality, and to calls for humanity. They offer an atheistic worldview both positive and guiding, and yes, faithful.

These writers present uneasy, contentious, complex, powerful, triumphant voices that allow goodness to shine without God. We remain uneasy with atheism in this country, as much as we profess freedom of religion—which we forget is also freedom *from* religion. The ways in which people raised in religious households, perhaps even among competing parental beliefs, find freedom in dismantling the oppressions of faith, become a liberating poetics as well. J. D. Schraffenberger's essay contains a series of bullet points under "Notes Towards an Atheist Poetics" which reads as an elegant manifesto for the atheist poet at work.

And now I shall make a profession of faithlessness. It seems required. As an atheist, I am not sure I can satisfy. I engage many Ojibwe practices as part of my way of living a good life, yet in my core understanding of the way of creation, I do not believe one all-powerful deity exists. To put is more directly, I have faith in and relation to creation itself rather than faith in a Creator.

Like the poets in this collection, my atheism, which I do not know I can even claim, was an evolution and is most apparent as I co-parent. We were both raised Catholic. We resisted the comforts of Catholicism when raising our two kids. When they were afraid, we reasoned. But we thought then, and many times in both our kids' childhoods, how easy would it be to just tell them God would always protect them? Or that God only made humans on earth and that there were no aliens in the Bible, so aliens do not exist. Watching *Signs*, I recalled that we told our son that any aliens that were out there were in a galaxy far, far away. We would probably see them coming for a hundred years. We thought we had told him the truth, but, watching *Signs* with its argument for faith in the face of alien invasion, I realized we had simply presented a belief system, physical science, as if it were fact in order to soothe a child. The many substitutions for religious faith are also part of this book and a part of my own poetry that I more clearly understand in light of this work.

Reading Jeremy Schraffenberger's "Notes" I have begun to look at how my own poems work within an aesthetic of atheism, even as they define spiritual connection in scientific terms. I hope that readers do the same and that broad audiences of all beliefs, or lack of belief, find this anthology an invitation to read poetry in light of atheism—because, these authors' work asserts, to do so is to follow a path toward a poetics of liberation, an expansion of worldview, and an understanding of what many people assume is impossible: what I call a good godlessness.

Heid E. Erdrich
June 22, 2016

The Necessary Poetics of Atheism

The Shiny Aluminum of God

Martín Espada

MANY YEARS AGO, I wrote an essay about my religious upbringing in Brooklyn, called "Argue Not Concerning God." (The title comes from Whitman's 1855 Preface to *Leaves of Grass*.) As I said in that essay:

I was raised by a Puerto Rican father and a Jewish-Jehovah's Witness mother. They met while working at the same factory in Brooklyn; my father was a shipping clerk, my mother a receptionist. Frank Espada was a skeptical, and lapsed, Catholic. Marilyn Levine ate cheeseburgers and expected to be bug-zapped by God for mixing meat and milk, in violation of dietary laws.

There is a context for her repudiation of the Jewish faith and identity, in favor of a proselytizing door-to-door Christian sect many people find more irritating than a case of ringworm. Sometime between her marriage to my father, in 1952, and my arrival, in 1957, my mother's family apparently disowned her. At age two, I glimpsed my mother's father, the only time I can remember meeting anyone in her family.

Boxed into the Linden projects of East New York, Brooklyn, with three children, my mother heeded a stranger at the door selling magazines and prophecy. During my father's absences, my siblings and I became, in effect, Witnesses as well. We learned that the Witnesses predicted "the end of this system of things," or Armageddon, a reference to the apocalypse, characterized in the magazines by pictures of crowds shrieking and cowering under a hail of fire. However, the Witnesses always chirped about "the good news" whenever they forecast the demise of the damned. After Armageddon came Paradise.

Illustrations of Paradise featured somnambulant beneficiaries of eternal life petting equally stupefied lions: Jehovah as taxidermist. The gardens were sterile, the faces numb with narcotic smiles. The Witnesses equated perfection with the deliberately bland, even when they sang. At an early age, I was convinced that their hymns were based on theme songs from television shows like "Gilligan's Island."

My father's arguments for atheism and evolutionary theory were ultimately persuasive. My mother's response to the theory of evolution was, "You may be descended from an ape, but I'm not." My mother's credibility also suffered when the Witnesses predicted "The End" for October 1975, and nothing ended but the baseball season.

. . . However, by the age of ten, I had already begun to question what I had learned from the Witnesses and the Bible.

THE OWL AND THE LIGHTNING
Brooklyn, New York

No pets in the projects,
the lease said,
and the contraband salamanders
shriveled on my pillow overnight.
I remember a Siamese cat, surefooted
I was told, who slipped from a window ledge
and became a red bundle
bulging in the arms of a janitor.

This was the law on the night
the owl was arrested.
He landed on the top floor,
through the open window
of apartment 14-E across the hall,
a solemn white bird bending the curtain rod.
In the cackling glow of the television,
his head swiveled, his eyes black.
The cops were called, and threw a horse blanket
over the owl, a bundle kicking.

Soon after, lightning jabbed the building,
hit apartment 14-E, scattering bricks from the roof
like beads from a broken necklace.
The sky blasted white, detonation of thunder.
Ten years old at the window, I knew then that God
was not the man in my mother's holy magazines,
touching fingertips to dying foreheads
with the half-smile of an athlete signing autographs.

God must be an owl, electricity
coursing through the hollow bones,
a white wing brushing the building.

My mother was not the only one in my household distributing spiritual reading material. My father introduced me to Omar Khayyám, the Persian poet, astronomer, mathematician, philosopher and mystic, and his "Rubáiyát" or quatrains, as translated by Edward FitzGerald.

Khayyám was a medieval poet (1048-1131) who rejected all the notions of God, heaven, hell, eternity and morality I had been taught. "Fools!" He cried. "Your Reward is neither Here nor There!" He went on:

Why, all the Saints and Sages who discuss'd
Of the Two Worlds so learnedly, are thrust
Like Foolish Prophets forth; their Words to scorn
Are scatter'd, and their Mouths are stopt with Dust.

Oh, come with old Khayyám, and leave the Wise
To talk; one thing is certain, that life Flies;
One thing is certain, and the Rest is Lies;
The Flower that once has blown for ever dies.

Khayyám and other discoveries in adolescence took me away from my religious upbringing.

The Playboy Calendar and
the Rubáiyát of Omar Khayyám

The year I graduated from high school,
my father gave me a Playboy calendar
and the *Rubáiyát* of Omar Khayyám.
On the calendar, he wrote:
Enjoy the scenery.
In the book of poems, he wrote:
I introduce you to an old friend.

The Beast was my only friend in high school,
a wrestler who crushed the coach's nose with his elbow,
fractured the fingers of all his teammates,
could drink half a dozen vanilla milkshakes,
and signed up with the Marines
because his father was a Marine.
I showed the Playboy calendar to The Beast
and he howled like a silverback gorilla
trying to impress an expedition of anthropologists.
I howled too, smitten with the blonde
called *Miss January*, held high in my simian hand.

Yet, alone at night, I memorized the poet-astronomer
of Persia, his saints and sages bickering about eternity,
his angel looming in the tavern door with a jug of wine,
his *battered caravanserai* of sultans fading into the dark.
At seventeen, the laws of privacy have been revoked
by the authorities, and the secret police are everywhere:
I learned to hide Khayyám and his beard
inside the folds of the Playboy calendar
in case anyone opened the door without knocking,
my brother with a baseball mitt or a beery Beast.

I last saw The Beast that summer at the Marine base

in Virginia called Quantico. He rubbed his shaven head,
and the sunburn made the stitches from the car crash years ago
stand out like tiny crosses in the field of his face.
I last saw the Playboy calendar in December of that year,
when it could no longer tell me the week or the month.

I last saw Omar Khayyám this morning:
Awake! He said. *For Morning in the Bowl of Night*
Has flung the Stone that puts the Stars to Flight.

Awake! He said. And I awoke.

There were other times in my adolescence when my father would find a way to pass along his heretical principles.

THE GODDAMNED CRUCIFIX
New York City, 1972

My father wandered through a dust storm in San Antonio
called diphtheria. By the time he stepped off the plane
in New York his windpipe was closing. The doctors in the city
could not recognize a disease dead as polio, killed off
by vaccination years ago. In the emergency room they said
drink this, and my father almost drowned in a glass of water.

Now many visitors came to pay homage on the ward
in the Catholic hospital, where the nurses and the crucifix
hovered over the bed. He did not want me there: *Don't let*
him see me like this, he said. I saw him: his black hair was white;
his brown skin was red; his ribs spread and his chest sank
with every rasping breath. He was skinny as a rubber chicken.

I leaned close to hear his last words, the dying wish I would
honor as his son for the rest of my life. And my father whispered:
Get that goddamned crucifix away from me. Honor thy father,

the Bible says, so I lifted Jesus off the nail on the wall
and hid Him in the drawer next to the bed, stuffed
back down into the darkness before the resurrection.

Only then did the miracle come to pass: my father lived.

A few years later, I left home and wandered all the way to Wisconsin. I dropped out of school, ran out of money, and was referred by a welfare agency to the local Christian charity, where I would be driven further in the direction of unbelief by the hypocrisy of the believers.

THE SAINT VINCENT DE PAUL FOOD PANTRY STOMP
Madison, Wisconsin, 1980

Waiting for the carton of food
given with Christian suspicion
even to agency-certified charity cases
like me,
thin and brittle
as uncooked linguini,
anticipating the factory-damaged cans
of tomato soup, beets, three-bean salad
in a welfare cornucopia,
I spotted a squashed dollar bill
on the floor, and with
a Saint Vincent de Paul food pantry stomp
pinned it under my sneaker,
tied my laces meticulously,
and stuffed the bill in my sock
like a smuggler of diamonds,
all beneath the plaster statue wingspan
of Saint Vinnie,
who was unaware
of the dance
named in his honor

by a maraca player
in the salsa band
of the unemployed.

    This brings me to "the Puerto Rican Christ": the spiritual symbol of an impoverished and colonized people. The image of Christ on the cross, deeply embedded in the culture and the consciousness, becomes an expression of loss, desperation, and abandonment. Indeed, the question Jesus asked on the cross—"Why have you forsaken me?"—is asked of *Him.*

    Driving through the mountain roads of the island, my father and I once encountered the image of a terribly vulnerable God, unable to protect anyone, even himself, a sacred symbol violated by those driven by hunger and hopelessness to commit an act of sacrilege. And so the "dark absence" of the Deity hung over us all.

THE SAVIOR IS ABDUCTED IN PUERTO RICO
Adjuntas, Puerto Rico, 1985

At a place in the mountains,
where the road skids
into tangled trees
and stacks of rock,
a single white cross leans.

The name has dissolved,
obscured in a century of storms
that asphyxiated shacks
with mud, yanking
the stone vertebrae
from bridges.

On the cross,
the dark absence of Christ
spreads and hangs,
a crucified shadow

where thieves
tore the brass body down,
leaving amputated feet and hands
still nailed,
and the accidental dead
without a guide
on the mountain roads
of the underworld.

The atheistic image of the Puerto Rican Christ may also become a vehicle of political protest. Such a protest, invoking Christ on the cross, raises questions: Who is crucified? Who is doing the crucifying? Who stands by and tacitly endorses the crucifixion? Who profits by it?

In Viejo San Juan, I witnessed a one-man protest against racism and police brutality using the symbolism of the Puerto Rican Christ.

CRUCIFIXION IN THE PLAZA DE ARMAS
Viejo San Juan, Puerto Rico 1998

By the fountain of statues in the plaza,
next to a sign where fractured letters protest torture by police,
a Black man stands shirtless and pinned to a cross arms wide
like the wingspan of a slave executed for trying to fly,
as high school students bounce to the tambourine
in plena improvisation and tourists from the trolley
crowd into the shop across the street
to search for carvings dark and sleek
as his scarred body, to hunt down their own Black Christ.

My grandmother died in Puerto Rico in 1997, and I traveled there for the funeral. The cousins I grew up with in New York had moved back to the island, and all had become *Pentacostales*: Protestant evangelicals.

Puerto Rico has been a colony of the United States since the Spanish-American War of 1898. Not by coincidence, it is the most Protestant country in Latin America. Here is a classic case of religion-as-opiate, and a poem where I express my anger at a God in whom I do not believe.

(*El pastor Pentecostal* is "the Pentecostal minister"; *la vida eterna* is "eternal life"; *Dios te ama* is "God loves you.")

The Shiny Aluminum of God
Carolina, Puerto Rico 1997

After the pilgrimage
to the Office of Cemetery Records,
we pay fifty dollars in cash
for the free municipal burial plot,
the clerk hiding the bills in a manila folder.
El pastor Pentecostal forgets the name of the dead,
points at the ceiling and gazes up
whenever he loudly whispers the syllables
for eternal life, *la vida etern*a,
as if the stain on the tile were the map of heaven.
The mourners are palm trees in the hallelujah wind,
hands raised overhead. Once grandmother Tata's pen
looped the words of the spirits as they spoke to her;
now she grips a borrowed golden crucifix
in the coffin, lid propped open by mistake.
The coffin bumps into a hole of mud
next to the chain-link fence, and then
the family Vélez Espada gathers for dinner.

The pernil is frozen, pork shoulder congealed and raw
like a hunk of Siberian woolly mammoth.
But Angela tells us of the miracle pot
that will roast the meat in an hour
without a cup of water. She sells the pot
to her neighbors too, keeps a tower of boxes
with a picture of the pot resplendent on every box.
The words on her kerchief hail
the shiny aluminum of God: *Dios te ama.*

The scar carves her husband's forehead
where the doctors scooped the tumor out,
where cancer cells scramble like a fistful of ants.
In a year he will be the next funeral, when the saints
of oncology surrender their weapons. For now
Edwin lives by the finches he snares in the backyard,
wings blundering through the trap door of the cage,
sold for five dollars apiece to the neighbors.
He praises God for brain surgery and finches,
leans close and grins about the time
his brother somersaulted out a window
and two swooping angels caught him
by the elbows, inches from the ground.
Only one broken rib, Edwin says,
rubbing his stomach in the slow way
of a man satisfied with his meal.
Angela's brother passes out pamphlets:
God's ambulance found him and his needle
in a condemned building, no shoes
and no heartbeat. Then Edwin says:
God will not let me die.

An hour later,
the pernil is still frozen in the oven.
Angela stares at the sweating pork,
then the boxes of pots unsold in the corner.
A boy cousin taps his fork
and asks if we can eat the finches.
The trap clatters in the backyard,
an angel flapping in the cage.

Where, then, does an atheist poet put his or her faith? Where do we find our salvation? Some poets would say: *Poetry.*

Sam Hamill would say that. Sam is a poet, translator, editor, activist and cofounder of Copper Canyon Press. He was born on an unknown date to unknown parents. Adopted in Utah, he was beaten and abused, a runaway, a petty thief, doing drugs, in trouble with the law, in and out of jail. In the poem, "Plain Dumb Luck," he writes of being

> huddled in a cell in Fredonia, Arizona
> rolling cigarettes from a Bull Durham pouch
> locked up for the crime of being fourteen and homeless.

A sheriff tells him to "Go home, son," yet:

> Home was the road
> for a kid whose other home was hell.
> I'd rather steal than taste that belt again.
> I stole.

And yet, by poem's end, forty years later, the poet concludes that he is "the luckiest son-of-a-bitch alive." It was his "dumb luck" to discover poetry. From the practice of poetry everything else would flow.

Poetry saved Sam Hamill. Poetry saved him from a life of violence, self-destruction and incarceration. I dedicated this poem to him.

BLASPHEMY
For Sam Hamill

> Let the blasphemy be spoken: poetry can save us,
> not the way a fisherman pulls the drowning swimmer
> into his boat, not the way Jesus, between screams,
> promised life everlasting to the thief crucified beside him
> on the hill, but salvation nevertheless.
>
> Somewhere a convict sobs into a book of poems
> from the prison library, and I know why
> his hands are careful not to break the brittle pages.

There is no doubt that religion and spirituality can provide the core principles of movements for progressive social change. Witness César Chávez and the United Farm Workers. Religion and spirituality can also influence the voice of a poet seeking social justice: the vocabulary, the motifs, the metaphors, and the vision. Sam Hamill himself is a Buddhist—and the founder of Poets Against the War.

There are also skeptics who nevertheless believe in the power of religious language and imagery. Jack Agüeros was the first poet I ever met, and my second father. He was the director of El Museo del Barrio, at the time the only Puerto Rican museum in the mainland United States. He was also a heretic who wrote psalms. This is his "Psalm for Distribution":

> Lord,
> on 8th Street
> between 6th Avenue and Broadway
> in Greenwich Village
> there are enough shoe stores
> with enough shoes
> to make me wonder
> why there are shoeless people
> on the earth.
>
> Lord,
> You have to fire the Angel
> in charge of distribution.

The poem addresses the Lord, but He is not the only audience. We must fire the Angel. We must radically transform this economic system so that everyone has shoes, and the opportunity to realize his or her full human potential. In the words of Walter Lowenfels: "When the tragedy of the world market no longer dominates our existence, new gradations of being in love with being here will emerge."

Yet the same heretical poet who wrote that irreverent psalm also organized an annual parade of camels, sheep and shepherds every January 6th—the *Día de Tres Reyes*, or Three Kings Day—through the streets of East Harlem. Agüeros understood the power of that ceremony in his community.

It would be untrue to say that I take nothing away from religion in general or the

Bible in particular. There is, for example, the following passage from the Book of Isaiah, chapter 2, verse 4:

> And they shall beat their swords into plowshares, and their spears into pruning hooks; nation shall not lift up sword against nation, neither shall they learn war any more.

The last poem takes this verse as a point of departure. There is a significant distinction between the utopian vision articulated in this poem and the Paradise of the Jehovah's Witnesses that terrified me in childhood. I believe in Galeano Utopianism.

This is Eduardo Galeano on utopia: "She's on the horizon . . . I go two steps closer, she moves two steps away. I walk ten steps and the horizon runs ten steps ahead. No matter how much I walk, I'll never reach her. What good is utopia? That's what: it's good for walking."

So we walk.

HEAL THE CRACKS IN THE BELL OF THE WORLD

For the community of Newtown, Connecticut, where twenty students and six educators lost their lives to a gunman at Sandy Hook Elementary School, December 14, 2012

Now the bells speak with their tongues of bronze.
Now the bells open their mouths of bronze to say:
Listen to the bells a world away. Listen to the bell in the ruins
of a city where children gathered copper shells like beach glass,
and the copper boiled in the foundry, and the bell born
in the foundry says: *I was born of bullets, but now I sing
of a world where bullets melt into bells.* Listen to the bell
in a city where cannons from the armies of the Great War
sank into molten metal bubbling like a vat of chocolate,
and the many mouths that once spoke the tongue of smoke
form the one mouth of a bell that says: *I was born of cannons,
but now I sing of a world where cannons melt into bells.*

Listen to the bells in a town with a flagpole on Main Street,
a rooster weathervane keeping watch atop the Meeting House,
the congregation gathering to sing in times of great silence.
Here the bells rock their heads of bronze as if to say:
Melt the bullets into bells, melt the bullets into bells.
Here the bells raise their heavy heads as if to say:
Melt the cannons into bells, melt the cannons into bells.
Here the bells sing of a world where weapons crumble deep
in the earth, and no one remembers where they were buried.
Now the bells pass the word at midnight in the ancient language
of bronze, from bell to bell, like ships smuggling news of liberation
from island to island, the song rippling through the clouds.

Now the bells chime like the muscle beating in every chest,
heal the cracks in the bell of every face listening to the bells.
The chimes heal the cracks in the bell of the moon.
The chimes heal the cracks in the bell of the world.

The Atheist in Holy Places

Lauren Marie Schmidt

WHEN I WAS HIRED to teach ninth-grade English at a Catholic high school in Oregon, I was asked to sign a "Morality Clause" as part of my contract, one that says that I would uphold the school's Catholic values, even though on the tour I took prior to my interview, I learned that less than half of the student body was Catholic. I remember studying the clause, trying to figure out what it meant and how it might change my decidedly Un-Catholic lifestyle: Would I have to start going to Church? Would I have to pray? Put up a Christmas tree? Dye Easter eggs?

These were not unfamiliar rituals to me. I was raised Catholic and, as a child, I had a profound sense of faith. I remember walking with my mother as she received Eucharist before I was of age, and saying grace at every meal. I remember how I cried from joy on the day I made my Confirmation. Even now, if I were to step in a church, I could recite large stretches of the Catholic Mass, word-for-word. I had moved randomly across the country to a city I'd never seen and I needed a job. I figured, too, that since I was raised Catholic, the Catholicness of the school wouldn't bother me, that I could, along with the other half of Non-Catholics, just grin and bear it through the Jesusy stuff.

But I wanted to be honest about the fact that I had moved to Oregon and was sharing an apartment with a man who would propose within the year. I asked if this would be grounds for termination since my boyfriend had not yet popped the question. "Are you going to marry this man?" Principal Perry asked. At the time, I wasn't lying when I said yes. Perry took me on board and I was relieved. I had been honest about my life and it didn't matter.

But on a Friday night in November of 2009, two and a half years after I'd called off that engagement, six months away from graduating from an M.F.A. program and my thirtieth birthday, five years after I balked at the language of that Morality Clause, and a new Principal later, I got fired from my job for writing a funny poem about a broken vibrator. When I moved back to my native New Jersey, I wrote the following poem:

Prayer for My Former Principal after Being Fired From My Catholic School Teaching Position for the Publication of a Poem about Masturbation

You just couldn't handle it, J—
the poem, or me, J, the rough-
mouthed Magdalene from Jersey
who skips Sunday Mass to gather
her rosebuds, who eats apples without
    washing them first.

I can just see you, J: three days
of praying, dropped on your knees
in your bedroom Gethsemane,
fingers wrung, white-knuckled.
Like an orb of unleavened bread,
locked palms are raised to night's sky.
Your wife's shapely, chalice-hips are stiff
with waiting beneath the shroud
of cotton sheets. But, no, J, you
are on your knees, halos flaming
in your finger-beds. I know you
    anoint yourself

on Sundays, J, fingers just dipped
in the holy dish, wet like my fingers wet
from my beating clit, but you know
how the poem goes. You can't sleep now
because of it. You pray, still pray
that you're a good man and wise,
everyday-devoted, pray you're humble
    before the only God

on high. Amen. Today, it is my turn
to say a prayer. I pray
that your wife uncrosses her legs,
folds my poem between the thighs
of her Bible, feeling the print that spells
a sin worth losing heaven. I pray
she shrinks away from you,
and flinches at your cold
and crooked fingers.

As much as I want to, I can't escape my religious upbringing. The images, the language, and the stories of my Catholic life—not to mention my post-secondary studies of Literature and Art History—are all so deeply rooted that they make their way into my work quite against my will. The same could be said for some of what people call "Catholic values."

If there's one thing Catholics got right, it's their commitment to service—although, I'd argue, of course, that service isn't an exclusively Catholic value, but it's one I don't mind tracing back to my Catholic roots—and this is where I found common ground with my colleagues. While living in Oregon, I volunteered at a family meals program for low-income and homeless families, a soup kitchen. The Dining Room, as it was called, was on my street, and I loved working there so much that I didn't mind being the on-call table busser when other volunteers failed to show. I found the work and the visitors so inspiring that I wrote my first book, *Psalms of The Dining Room*, about what I witnessed there and in the homeless community around my city.

For a long time, I labored over the title. I wanted to avoid sounding religious, though I preferred *Psalms* to *Songs of The Dining Room*. I preferred it, I think, because there was something holy about that place and those people, the interactions we shared, the energy of the work, and the word "Songs" simply wouldn't have cut it. There is, unavoidably, religious imagery and language all over that book—so much, in fact, that when I read my poems aloud, people automatically assume I have "a very strong faith." Here is one such example:

PRAYER

For Jeremy and The Dining Room, Eugene, Oregon

When I clear your table after you've gone, there's a small scrap
of paper which reads: "God Bless You. You are Beautiful.
I Promise to Pray for You." *Pray* for me? Pray for *me*?
Then pray for me that I wake up in the morning in a bed
and lie there, that I give my blessings their proper names
and faces, the blessings that keep me from a life too like
yours, pray for me. Because the first thought of my day

is hunger, pray for me that I eat. But pray for me that I know
hunger, pray for me. Pray for me that I feel myself in
the growl of your belly, that I remember I am more like you
than I remember, pray for me. Pray for me that I am Rodney
with his weary eyes who is all at once teacher, cousin,
neighbor, friend, and the stranger who held the door for me
when my arms were full of bags, please pray. Pray for me
that I am the woman with earth-rich skin. Pray for those hands
that slammed her plate face-down into the table for me to clean.
Pray for me that I know no such grief, pray for me.
Pray for me that I am Larry whose fingers shoot music
into the belly of the piano; those same seven songs spark
from its upright head. Pray for me that I have the comfort
of knowing what comes next, pray for me. Pray for me that I am

the blind man because the room knows to make room for him.
People move tables, chairs, themselves, part a path for him as if
he were a king. But pray for me that I make way, pray for me.

Pray for me that I am Amber with her Vaseline face,
whose words are frenzied centipedes that scatter from her lips
and braid above her head. She stares at them like a mobile
or a noose. She stares at them like she would a heaven. Pray for me

there's a heaven. That the demons tattooed along Leanne's spine
do not exist, pray for me. Pray for me that my back can carry
such blackness if it needs to, pray for me. Pray for me that I am
the pregnant girl who is allowed a second plate. Pray that I know
the power I hold in my body, for a tiny king can grow eyes in my body,

please pray. Pray for me that I am the man in this same room, seated
at another table, the man that gives the girl his milk. Pray for me
that I remember to give up my milk. Pray for me that I am the milk.

Sure, given the title and the repetition of the phrase "pray for me," I can see why people might assume I'm religious. But if they do, they missed what is absolutely essential to the poem. The poem is not about my prayer—it's about Jeremy's. I express very clearly my skepticism in the first stanza: "*Pray* for me? Pray for *me?*"

I've always been fascinated by the fact that people who appear to be in the direst of circumstances often have the deepest faith. So I ask, "Pray for ME?" as a way of pointing out that if one of the two of us is in need of prayers, it certainly isn't me. And even though I don't pray myself, I respect that it means a lot to people who do, so I launch into all the things about the Dining Room worth praying for. Certainly, there are many.

Unlike some of the people who come across my work, I see my poems as much more political than religious. My activism is not a Get-out-of-Hell or Get-into-Heaven free card because I don't believe in either. I choose to work with some of the most disenfranchised people in our society—the homeless, women on welfare, men and women in recovery, at-risk youth, illiterate adults—because I have been (forgive the terminology here) very blessed in my life—not by some God, but by my blue-collar, working-class parents, by the teachers I have had in my life, by the company I keep now. And maybe that's why I feel safe in a world where I don't believe there's a God: the notion of God simply isn't necessary. I have something better. My work explores the ways in which my family life has both shaped and challenged my belief in God.

Receiving

My mother used to share wads of peanut butter
off a spoon with our dog, and I couldn't get over
           how to drink blood from a chalice with a church-
ful of strangers. The little napkin ministers used
to pinch the drink's rim clean was not a suitable

measure of preventative health, so I'd fall in line
behind my mother whose mouth was indiscriminately
           faithful, who once ate the host off the floor after it fell
from an old woman's lips, tongue-slicked side down,
no doubt, wet with a stranger's spit, the mist

of a stranger's prayer. When I asked my mother why
she didn't pick up the host and give it to the woman, why
           she pressed it to her tongue and crossed herself instead,
she said, *It would have been a sin not to receive it*
the way it had been given to me. I always cupped my hands,

held them out for the offering—my faith neatly packaged,
delivered in a way I could understand, though its message
           wholly lost on me, especially on Sunday evenings,
when our priest came to our house to give my stroke-broken
grandfather Communion. I'd watch him labor to follow

the priest's prayers—a series of babbles and the occasionally
well-landed Amen—before Father O'Brien would place
           the round wafer on Grandpa's tongue, lift blood
to Grandpa's lips. Only old people opened their mouths
for the Eucharist. I remember being told that the way

to receive Christ's body was not to chew it, but to push
the unleavened flesh with my tongue to the roof of my mouth
           until it dissolved there, but in our kitchen—

Christ's house everywhere—Grandpa would chomp the body,
which seemed appropriate for a man with this body: dead

right arm, dead right leg, limbs like crosses he dragged through
more than two decades before dying, not many words other than
        shit, fuck, goddammit, and *douchebag.* My father told me that,
as the soon-to-be new man of Grandpa's house, he sent away one
of Grandpa's sisters from the kitchen days after his stroke for laughing

at him crying, trying to make words, and fumbling a fork
with his left hand. We three kids came not long after,
        and in family pictures, Grandpa holds us tightly on his left leg,
snug in the crook of his left arm like little pink footballs.
There are Christmas pictures, pictures of him leaning over,

laughing because he's about to fart, pictures of us kissing him
on the lips, the way the next generation of kids kiss us
        on the lips now, but there is an age when this will change,
when the children will twist spastically away, swat at our lips,
or run for cover. *The only kiss on the lips my father ever gave me*

as a woman, my mother once said, *was on my wedding day.*
There is a picture of this in our house, a slightly side-of-the-lips
        kiss because my mother, a bride of just twenty, didn't know
how to receive it, what would be the last kiss from her father while
he was still well on what was to be her last day in her father's house,

but two years later, she would return to her father's house,
her three children born and raised in her father's house. And though
        she does not say this, my mother wishes she had not
half-refused her father's kiss—she keeps that pang pressed
to the roof of her mouth, waiting for it to dissolve.

When I returned to New Jersey, I began a poetry workshop at a transitional housing program for homeless, unwed mothers. I served there for nearly two years while in graduate school before I moved again for a full-time teaching position. In many ways, this service was more personal than my service at The Dining Room not only because of the time I spent with these ten women, but how we spent that time: reading and writing poetry. On the other hand, I was consistently confronted with the fact that this particular institution—whose name I've changed in the poems I've written—seemed to be at odds with its own mission to transform these women's lives so that they are self-sufficient. I wrote the following poem in response to this glaring disparity:

THE SOCIAL WORKER'S ADVICE
The Haven House for Homeless Women and Children

Jabbing a finger at my face, you say, *You can't have*
empathy. Empathy will eat you alive, as if empathy
were a beast with feathers, fur, and hair, with hind legs
and deft feet, wings and claws, a beast that soars,
stalks, lunges, springs, a beast that chases, a beast
that screams instead of sings, with giant jaws
and a tongue budded with a rapacious taste for fools
like me, fools who don't believe the beast exists to eat,
who let it burrow its snout between our legs, fingers,
up to our armpits—the spaces of our common human stink.

But you see a beast that sniffs and snarls for a thick blue vein
to sic, and when I look at you I understand the beast more plainly—
I see that its skin collects pock marks each time you dock
merit points to teach the mothers not to "talk Black,"
I see that its forehead sprouts a thousand of your scornful eyes,
its claws slash as swift and deep as your condescension—

because what you mean is that I can't have empathy
for these girls, for times like these, for a place like this,
for Nicole who tallies the number of days it's been
since she last flushed her veins with a spoon-cooked mix,

twenty-eight days and counting. No empathy
for Nicole because she can never seem to find
matching socks for her four-year-old son, or because
she folds flowers from twice-used computer paper
to calm her nerves. Bouquets of paper daisies
sprout from vases on all four tables in the dining room.

What you mean is that I can't have empathy for Takina,
who was told to go by Tina because her white, adoptive
mother—middle-aged, middle-classed—prefers it.
Her birth-mother is five years gone and Tina-Takina
thinks she might be pregnant again. I can't have empathy

for Denice who is pregnant with her third, but didn't know
until she was too far in, for Angelica who fell down the stairs
while holding her infant son, too spent from pre-sun
feedings and weeping in the wee hours as minutes lurch by.
Each tick-tock is the sound of the dead-locked door
of the nighttime aide who snores in the small room
near the exit like a beast at the gates, preventing escape
from this place, this time, from lives like these
without signing a release form for the Division of Youth
and Family Services, like Dionna, who took her two kids
to a hotel where, alone, at night, she stares at ceiling holes
in the red glow of the word VACANCY flashing through
windows with no curtains. I can't have empathy for LaQuita,
so thin that when she aims her breast at her baby's lips,
she prays she has something wet and real to give.

When you say, with your wagging finger, *You can't have*
empathy. Empathy will eat you alive, what you mean
is that I can't have empathy for these girls, and when I look
at you, I cannot help but wonder when you first believed
empathy would do more than sniff and lick your palms.

So, I say, let it take me, then, this beast of your invention,
let it slip its fangs into my skin and tear through my throat,
let it suck all the fat and blood from off my solid bones.

In spite of, or likely because of the kind of treatment these women received from the staff on a daily basis, these young mothers had to find their own ways to defend their humanity, their dignity.

CLOISTERED
The Haven House for Homeless Women and Children

There are no men in the Haven House.
And whether it was the tides and the moon

or the nearness of their rooms, ten red rosaries
aligned, and the animal throb of their bodies

too hard for two mothers to deny, so when
I say, *Write a poem about a body you know*—

bodies of their sons, their daughters,
their mothers, their own—Shauna writes

of the night she made her way into a bedroom
down the hall, and reads aloud her poem

about the dark vinegar of another woman's
menstruation on her mouth, the tang of that

first forbidden taste. She reads about how
the scent of red-brown silt streaked her nose,

chin, and cheeks, how her fingernails carried
crescents of blood for three days before the smell

they held was fully scrubbed away, how she'd lift
her fingers to her nose to inhale, teasing her secret

lover in the hallways and over dinner. But here
she is now, the door to her confessional wide open.

All other mothers but one are scared. Of what,
it is not clear: the blood, the body, two bloods,

two bodies, sex at all in a place where you can't
even snack in the living room, sex because

sex put them here in the first place, though
not this sex, hidden sex, between-two-

women sex, at that-time-of-the-month sex,
with-the-nighttime-aide-just-downstairs sex,

there-are-no-men-in-the-Haven-House sex,
so two women turned to each other, bowed

to the cross of the other woman's body,
and drank deeply of her consecrated wine.

One of the hardest things for me to reconcile is the fact that, despite the Separation of Church and State, religion, particularly factions of Christianity, often plays a huge part in the political debates in our country. Too many politicians rely on moral platforms, wedge issues—things like gay marriage and abortion—to earn their seats at the public table; yet, they are the very same people who have the least amount of compassion and empathy for the victims of our political and economic systems. I confront this issue in the following poem:

UNTO OTHERS
To the Roomful of People at the Private Fundraiser
for Mitt Romney, May 2012

"There are 47 percent who are with [the President], who are dependent upon government, who believe that they are victims, who believe that government has a responsibility to care for them, who believe that they are entitled to health care, to food, to housing, to you name it. . . . That's entitlement."
—Mitt Romney

"All things therefore whatsoever ye would that men should do unto you, even so do ye also unto them."
—Matthew 7:12

"Who is here so vile that will not love his country? If any, speak; for him have I offended."
—*Julius Caesar*, Act II, scene ii

Who there knows how good it is to know
a warm bed and a roof? If any, speak.

Who there knows how good it is to know
a schoolroom? If any, speak.

Who there knows how good it is to know
the stiffness of new shoes? If any, speak.

Who there knows how good it is to know
the steam of a meal on your cheeks? If any, speak.

Who there knows how good it is to know
some God hears you weep? If any, speak.

Who there knows how good it is to know?
All of you know, so speak.

Say you know how good it is to know.
All of you know, so speak. Say it's OK

for others to know how good it is to know.
Say it. Speak. You lose nothing

if others know how good it is to know.
Go ahead. Speak.

If you know how good it is to know,
why then don't you speak?

Why then don't you speak?
Say something. Speak. Speak. Speak.

This poem is part of my forthcoming collection: *Filthy Labors* (Curbstone/Northwestern University Press). Despite my atheism, this manuscript does not escape my Catholic past either! In fact, the entire structure is based upon the seven sacraments, a series of Christian rituals including things like Baptism, Communion, and Confirmation. But instead of using Bible passages on the title pages of each section, I use quotes from Whitman's *Leaves of Grass*.

Whitman was a skeptic. At least. But anyone can look at Whitman's body of work and make a reasonable case that he did have some kind of faith in God. And sometimes, he, too, questions whether or not the notion of God is even important. "Argue not concerning God," he says, but also this:

O Me! O Life!

Oh me! Oh life! of the questions of these recurring,
Of the endless trains of the faithless, of cities fill'd with the foolish,
Of myself forever reproaching myself, (for who more foolish than I, and who more faithless?)
Of eyes that vainly crave the light, of the objects mean, of the struggle ever renew'd,

Of the poor results of all, of the plodding and sordid crowds I see around me,
Of the empty and useless years of the rest, with the rest me intertwined,
The question, O me! so sad, recurring—What good amid these, O me, O life?

Answer.
That you are here—that life exists and identity,
That the powerful play goes on, and you may contribute a verse.

Though Whitman's faithlessness is up for debate, his goodness isn't. There are few poets whose work preserves and celebrates the dignity of human life the way Whitman does, so whether he believes in God or not becomes secondary to the one thing that is undeniable about him: He is good.

The same could be said of Mother Teresa, right? She was good. But was she faithful? In the years I was living in Oregon—an Atheist teaching in a Catholic school, volunteering for the homeless a few times a week, writing seemingly religious poems that will be published by a Catholic press—there were several articles surrounding Mother Teresa's apparent skepticism.

In 2009, a book of her writings was published: *Mother Teresa: Come Be My Light: The Private Writings of the Saint of Calcutta.* In it, she writes: "I call, I cling, I want ... and there is no One to answer . . . no One on Whom I can cling . . . no, No One. Alone . . . Where is my Faith . . . even deep down right in there is nothing, but emptiness & darkness . . . My God . . . how painful is this unknown pain . . . I have no Faith . . . I dare not utter the words & thoughts that crowd in my heart . . . & make me suffer untold agony. . . . I try to raise my thoughts to Heaven. There is such convicting emptiness that those very thoughts return like sharp knives & hurt my very soul. I am told God loves me . . . and yet the reality of darkness & coldness & emptiness is so great that nothing touches my soul."

I was so moved by the fact that in spite of her faithlessness, she still did the work, and after reading her letters, I wanted to understand her loss, since my own loss of faith was not as painful as she describes in her private writings.

MOTHER TERESA, OUR DEARLY BELOVED MOTHER

they chipped into my stone chest, but little
else to say I soldiered for Christ. Badged,
I lived my life in the name of Christ, stormed
faithless troops on the frontlines for Christ.
Heavier is stone than wood. The Word,
        heavier still. And now,

when wind cuts across the letters' trenches
of my name, I hear the prayers that long since
        have fallen from my tongue.

For, in the evenings' darkest hours—
from when clock hands clasp upward in prayer
to the moments before morning's Christ
again rises—I looked up and saw
        not God, but nothing.

Tired of having this and other more overtly Atheist poems praised by editors and then promptly rejected, I stopped sending them out. This poem has been sitting in a drawer for more than five years, and I still won't send it out because as far as we've come—there are poets writing about sex, prejudice, and other push-the-envelope subjects—Godlessness is still taboo. There are no nationally-recognized journals dedicated exclusively to Atheist poetry, and the regional ones, often online, are so poor that it's difficult, even as an Atheist, to take them seriously. I began my M.F.A. program in the summer of 2008 and since then, I've been paying attention: There aren't any notable anthologies dedicated to Atheist poetry. None of the big-name journals—*The Ploughshares*, *The Kenyon Reviews*, and certainly not *The New Yorkers*—even risk producing a themed issue on the subject. And AWP, an organization that accepts topics like Poetry and Yoga for the annual conference, hasn't permitted panels on Atheist poetry either. I still write Atheist poetry, but I understand the cost of doing so.

In the winter of 2009, just before I returned to New Jersey to live with my 92-year-old grandfather, poor, jobless and humiliated, a married couple I worked with sent me to a monastery in the Oregon woods for four days so that I could, in some way, make peace with the betrayal I'd suffered there. On my first night, one of the head monks died. My friends joked that my presence is what sent him over the edge, ya know, because of my atheism. I attended the monks' prayer service every night. I ate in communion with strangers who were there for their own reasons in silence—no talking in the monastery. I wrote poetry. I slept. I hiked. I cried. I read nothing but Hafiz, and even I, a heathen, can appreciate him:

I HAVE LEARNED SO MUCH

I
Have
Learned
So much from God
That I can no longer
Call
Myself

A Christian, a Hindu, a Muslim,
A Buddhist, a Jew.

The Truth has shared so much of Itself
With me

That I can no longer call myself
A man, a woman, an angel,
Or even pure
Soul.

Love has
Befriended Hafiz so completely
It has freed me

Of every concept and image
My mind has ever known.

WHAT TRUTH IS TO BE HAD:
AN ATHEIST POETICS

———

J. D. SCHRAFFENBERGER

THE INTREPID TITLE of this book alludes to Percy Shelley's infamous 1811 pamphlet *The Necessity of Atheism*, the publication of which resulted in his being expelled from Oxford University—no great loss for the young rebellious poet, who reassures his father that he is "perfectly indifferent to the late tyrannical proceedings at Oxford." Later, he complains to William Godwin that "Oxonian society was insipid to me, uncongenial with my habits of thinking." Shelley's "habits of thinking" are ours—unavoidably—as we are all heirs to the Romantics: free and open inquiry, independent thought, imaginative truth-seeking.

The substance of *The Necessity of Atheism* was hardly groundbreaking in its claims, even then, as he is really only rehearsing the arguments of Locke and Hume; we remember Shelley—rightly—for different reasons, but his atheism nevertheless did inform his larger poetics because of its insistence on unfettered, unenslaved thought and feeling. And atheism can—indeed *should*—still inform our own poetics today. The project continues: to liberate our minds, to remove the chains of convention, the veil of superstition.

Shelley attributes the epigraph of *The Necessity of Atheism* to Bacon's great *De Augmentis Scientarium*: "Quod clara et perspicua demonstratione careat pro vero habere mens omino nequis humana," in English "The human mind can never accept as true that which lacks clear and evident proof." Quite simply, he argues for atheism on the grounds that there is no convincing evidence for the existence of a god. Instead, we should believe our senses, our experiences, or (if they are guided by reason) the experiences of others. This argument is what Shelley means by "necessary": if there is no proof, then atheism is the necessary corollary. Today, however, his argument seems rather dusty and banal, lacking both the rhetorical sophistication and the passionate *umph* of the New Atheists. By "necessary," I intend something slightly different and less metaphysical. The root sense of the word suggests something that we should not back away from, avoid, evade, something we must instead face. Atheism is still a dangerous word in the twenty-first century, just as it was back in the nineteenth. As Shelley explains to his friend Edward Trelawny, "atheist"

> is a word of abuse to stop discussion, a painted devil to frighten the foolish, a threat to intimidate the wise and good. I used it to express my abhorrence of superstition; I took up the word, as a knight took up a gauntlet, in defiance of injustice. The delusions of Christianity are fatal to genius and originality: they limit thought.

The necessity of atheism for me, then—and I hope for my poetic contemporaries—is to encourage discussion, to avoid superstition, to defy injustice, to cultivate genius and originality, to liberate thought, to argue for the contemporary cultural urgency for atheist artists—like Shelley before us—to acknowledge how their lack of religious belief informs their creative lives. For these reasons, I use Shelley as a point of departure, reaching back to him as a prominent poetic forebear who was unafraid to announce his atheism and unafraid to write explicitly atheist poems.

I hope to demonstrate—or at least suggest—how a poetics of atheism can be seen at work in my own writing—sometimes very subtly and not unambiguously—and then to offer by way of ending a few notes toward an atheist poetics, leaving up for discussion what the further implications of such a poetics might be.

My two books of poetry, *Saint Joe's Passion* (Etruscan Press) and *The Waxen Poor* (Twelve Winters Press), both bear distinctly Christian titles. The former refers not to the Joseph of the Bible but rather to the fictional Joseph Johnstone, erstwhile classical music public radio show host, who also performed voice-over work for commercials. The poems are inspired by Bach's oratorio *Saint Matthew Passion* as they tell Joseph's story after his diagnosis of throat cancer. The poem "Magnetism" from the early pages of *Saint Joe's Passion* describes his struggles more or less explicitly:

Magnetism

Joseph suffers conversation and longs
      for sleep: this is the great tragedy of his life.
    There are so many other minor tragedies besides.
What some mistake for wisdom or simply shyness
      or sheer stupidity is in fact a deep and lasting
        lack of faith—a bond with his disbelief.
    And like magnets coming together, the bond grows
stronger the closer he comes to it. One day,
      not long ago, during the seventh take of a cell phone
        spot, the magnet of his disbelief clicked onto his heart,
    and he walked out of the studio, aware that
someday very soon all of his previous ties would
    unravel. *Maybe he just needs a break. Maybe he needs*
        to be alone. It's unlike Joe to be so . . . unprofessional.

The narrative arc of *Saint Joe's Passion*, as this poem hints at, is Joseph's crisis of faith, "the magnet of his disbelief" intensifying until he finally leaves his former life behind. This book is a direct treatment of the first (sometimes) difficult glimmers of atheism as they shed some tentative light on the world around us. In some ways I identify with Joseph as a character, but in many important ways I do not. He is timid, fearful, pained by his atheism and barely able to admit it, even to himself. I've been an unashamed atheist since childhood.

The following poem, "How Many at Last?" begins with a clearly recognizable Christian scene but is soon transformed from being a love poem into a deeper philosophical meditation on salvation, as the poet moves from garden to desert to an emptied and demystified sky. Ultimately, what will save us is "two lips, a tongue," not a kiss but human speech itself.

HOW MANY AT LAST?

after Catullus' Poem 7

"My Lesbia, you ask how many kisses
would be enough to satisfy, to sate me!"

One of death at the garden gate, as Judas
gave discreet on the cheek at Gethsemane.

And one of life, unreturned, as upon the cold
rubber-doll lips of the coy Resusci Annie.

And one, if you will, for the wild heart's ease,
twice more in the post-op ring before I rise.

And again as many as the grains of white
Chihuahuan sand, agave scrub, the alluvial

evergreen fan. As many as the tarbush bloom,
the yucca, the whitethorn, the tall desert spoon.

Out here, cracking desert crust with our toes,
we are waiting for a lost love's return.

We gawk, we gape, silent and duned, but too few
stars gaze down at these common human desires.

We are mad, unloved dummies, opened to the sky,
uncounted by what will save us, two lips, a tongue.

The title of my second book comes from Leviticus: "And if thy brother be waxen poor, and fallen in decay with thee; then thou shalt relieve him: yea, though he be a stranger, or a sojourner; that he may live with thee." Leviticus can't be said to contain the most enlightened bits of wisdom from the Christian Bible (sanctioning as it does human slavery), but I read *this* passage, at least, as a call to help others who are suffering as their poverty grows (waxen poor), even those who are perhaps indebted to us (fallen in decay with thee). This book is about the poet's younger brother, who has suffered from mental illness since his diagnosis of schizophrenia. The poems in *The Waxen Poor*, then, are themselves an attempt to "relieve him . . . so that he may live with thee." The following poem connects the paranoid logic of psychosis with religious belief, specifically the "delusions of Christianity," which Shelley said are "fatal to genius and originality."

PARANOIA

So my Pentecostal preacher grandfather says
The troubles of our world keep getting worse
And worse, Cain keeps killing Abel, over and
Over, the wicked striking the righteous down.

And my brother says the world is out to get him
Agents of danger following him to the store
To buy a pack of smokes, peeking in windows
At night, jotting down notes on his dreams.

So Cain comes knocking at my brother's door
To sell him a set of encyclopedias, the world's
Knowledge (all of it!) there for him to peruse.
Just think, my boy, you could learn to be a god!

Then Cain comes to my grandfather's church,
Praises Jesus like a pro, sings songs of longing
To be born again in the sweet bosom of the Lord.
Just think, Brother, I could be saved at last!

So my brother finally becomes a god of his own
Desire and devising. He looks into the humdrum
Happenings of the world and sees the strange,
The telling, the beautiful and therefore true.

And my grandfather dunks Cain's big head deep
In a bath of Christian love, shouts I have saved
The world at last! forgiven the beastliest brother
Of 'em all! It's time now to lie out in the sun to dry.

Now I find my brother lying on his nappy couch
With his head in the lap of his new brother Cain,
Who reads him entries on Dream, Sleep, Death.
I listen hard, try to understand, but am not able.

While "Paranoia" is explicitly anti-religious, the next poem from *The Waxen Poor* makes a subtler case for how we might find truth in the world. Instead of relying on epiphany as a means of discovery, we should observe the material world, look to our very bodies and the senses that guide them, for meaning.

EPIPHANY

It was more like understanding, the way
Our legs under-stand us, the way the lung
Understands air, the pupil light, the tongue
What is sweet.
        There was no grace by god,
No sudden radiance.
           Light came, if it came,
Slowly, and what appeared appeared as though
There were no odds against appearing at all.

It was, Ah so the ocean comes and goes,
Leaving traces of its way, as do we all,
In spirals of debris.
        It was, Ah now I see:
Truth dawdles out the inevitable day.

True understanding does not require "sudden radiance"—or as Martín Espada writes in his own poem called "Epiphany" from his collection *The Trouble Ball* (2012), "Epiphany is not a blazing light." Instead of "radiance" or "blazing light," the truth comes to us in modest "spirals of debris," if only we pay attention, if only we learn to read, interpret, or otherwise understand the world.

The next poem, "Bad Luck," pokes fun at superstitious ideas, beliefs, and behaviors that often inform religious faith: a lighthearted expression of "my abhorrence of superstition," as Shelley puts it.

Bad Luck

It's bad luck to say or spell your name backward
Unless of course you do so while looking into a mirror,
And then only if the mirror isn't scratched or cracked,
And only if it's not midnight, or February 29th, or your birthday.
But I'm sure you know that already. (To be safe you should just avoid
Saying or spelling your name backward at all, even as a joke.)

It's also bad luck to forget to trim one of your nails,
When you're trimming your nails, unless you or someone
In the same room—or your mother, your father, or a sibling—
Is missing a finger. Some think it's bad luck to be missing a finger,
But those people are insensitive and superstitious.

Swallowing any coin is bad luck unless you find it
Once you've passed it, in which case, it's tremendously good luck. (Yay!)
But it's bad luck—obviously the worst luck of all—
To spend a coin that you've swallowed, passed, and subsequently found.
To receive such a coin in a monetary transaction
Has no bearing whatsoever on your luck.

It's bad luck to have a medical procedure on your birthday.
This doesn't include dental work. (Don't worry about dental work
On your birthday.) But dreams in which you are able some how to speak
A foreign language that you are not actually able to speak
In your awake life are bad luck unless you're having that dream
On your birthday, and then it's good luck (all right!) because it means
You'll eventually learn to speak that or a related language fluently.

A lot of things people dream about used to be bad luck,
Like eating something that isn't food, or becoming someone else,
Or falling asleep while you're already asleep and then waking up again and again,
But for the most part now it's safe to go ahead and dream
Whatever it is you dream without worrying about
How it will affect your luck or the luck of anyone around you.

Everybody knows it's bad luck to fall asleep at a funeral,
But did you know that it's worse luck to *sneeze* at a funeral?
In fact, there's a lot of stuff you should definitely not do at funerals.
In general, I'd recommend laying pretty low when someone you know dies.

It remains bad luck, just so you know, to predict
How the world will end (fire, ice, et cetera) when it's obvious really
That it ends the same way every time.

"Bad Luck" dwells on anxieties of the body, specifically mortality, which is always at the root of even the most mundane of superstitions. The etymology of the word itself reveals this fear of death: *super* + *stare* in Latin means to stand over, to survive. In superstition, we stand over our own bodies, in illusory control of mortality.

The next two thoroughly materialist poems also dwell in the body, insisting on the senses as the location of our primary experiences of the world and therefore the first place to seek truth, meaning, understanding.

SKY BURIAL

I wish my bones were with theirs.
—Robinson Jeffers

All religions want you
To vanish,
At least the body parts
Of you.

*

J. D. Schraffenberger

Up here, in the cold
Thinning dawn,
You're alms
For the monastery birds.

*

The body breakers come
To flay you
And pound your wet bones
Into paste.

*

The last bit
Is gone,
And someone sings a song
You've never heard before.

Sky burial is the ritual funeral practice in Tibet of dissecting and leaving corpses on a mountaintop, exposing them to the elements and to scavenging animals; the Tibetan word for sky burial, jhator, means "the giving of alms to the birds." The poem asks us to think deeply about our bodies and what happens when "the last bit" of us is gone.

AIRPORT

They usher us forth in lines—TSA—they smoke
In Detroit crannies. Red leather purses, a book
Of blue matches, baggies of cream, of paste and gel,
The disclosure and declaration of all things metallic.

They don't know what to make of Whitman's
Ribb'd breast, stashed, luggage-borne, his heart (ho)
Heaving within. They poke with plastic pointers,
Illuminating caverns with a penlight, swoosh round

And round with magic wands, and sign finally off
On its fitness for flight. This the port of petty poets,
A strapping tight of sashes, the spondaic click of heels.
They beep and butt against us, Terminal A, Terminal B,

Wherever is to be found the desperate hustle of air.
On speakers and screens they tell us, sgraffitied in stalls
They plead. Where to go, where to go, Terminal C.
A quick stub of Sbarro calzone, a Brookstone massage,

We grub, we stretch and breathe cold fluorescent air.
It's February, or March, an early morning song, late evening
Croon, and saw palms in pots peek past the shoulders
Of Tampa entrepreneurs. This the floral port of plenty,

Leap Year, twilight shadow in yellowed-over clouds.
The tall Poet in his green tweed coat, a thick white
Sweep of hair blown back under the automatic AC,
Hassled by security over proper ID. Forget blood, he says

Forget bone. The joists of life are laid on the winds,
Gust and breeze as they please. The cycles wheel,
The cycles wheel, and the whoosh and whistle of his words
Remind us of unintentional elegy, angels of our anti-world.

Take it to the streets, down alleys and gutters. Take it
Circling cul-de-sacs under a sheen of Ontario snow.
But take it. Brother of the trashbin wheels, O Father
Of the plastic fork, take a seat, wipe your brow,

Unfurl your roll of sacks for us. What else might you
Contain? After we are gone, there will be what you contain.
They bully to belief, they appease. The ticket-taker's
Ennui smile, the flashlight flasher's goggled stare,

The captainly tenor of pater noster smooth—this,
These, and more will be contained. Light, water,
Bone. Earth, mind, sky. Elemental trinities
Unframed at last, the hwæt and lo of holy quietude.

Your girlish giggle, your boyish braggadocio,
Your glance and stare fixed me unbuckled
To the seat—I admit it, yes, I've only been
Half-listening all along, the pompous prof

At thirty-thousand feet. This the port of pallid cheek.
This the port of seemliness and apology. Dixie-whistlers,
All of us, in the ravenous dark, lovers till landing,
What ends may come, neither here nor there,

Clock-stopped manglers of many tongues, of breath
Borne and air, we heave inside our bodies home.

While "Sky Burial" prompts us to consider what happens to our bodies when we die, "Airport" offers new ways to live: finding "Elemental trinities" that are "Unframed" by religious belief. We're left with "Light, water, / Bone. Earth, mind, sky," not to worship but to ponder in "holy quietude." Similarly, the next poem, "The First Person," repositions religious impulses, trying to discover something more elemental, more ancient, more fundamentally human, more true. It's dedicated to Mitochondrial Eve, the most recent common matrilineal ancestor of all humans, who lived 100,000 to 200,000 years ago.

THE FIRST PERSON

for Mitochondrial Eve

Whatever breed, whatever formal or informal
Arrangement of gestures of face, however
Many fingers or hands might reach, or lips,
The size of the holes of her eyes and nose,
Whatever words or uttered sound, whatever
Likeness unto each, whatever birth and forgetting
Where old rivers go or once went, whatever
Taste of whatever blood still coiling inside,
Whoever you have to fool, bribe, cheat, kill,

Find her and tell her something grave again
Has happened, here the last nerve, angle of repose,
Tell her we'll be waiting up all night on the roof
Listening in the dark for the light of her voice and
What to do, what to do now, what to do, what to do.

Reaching back in time through history and into our pre-historic past can replace the idea of a god who created us—not as ancestor worship, but as a way to retain something of the awe and wonder of human existence that religion sometimes engenders. The vastness of the universe, the age of our planet, the evolution of humans as thinking creatures—these facts are more inspiring, more awesome, more wondrous than a sky father who created us out of clay could ever be. The next poem takes on the idea of just such a sky father.

Sine Nomine Patris

I will call you Lily Gilder
Turing Tester Half-Crazed Muttnik
I will call you Brady Buncher
Shark Jumper Exerciser of Desire
Yes you will be Baywatcher
You will be Space Ghoster Holy
Roller Jayhawker Sandbagger
I will call you Maginot Liner
Cracker Jacker I will call you
Velvet Fogger Backroads Traveller
I will say Big League Chewer
Wiffle Baller O Blue Moon Sinner
I will call your true name
And you will answer Shoegazer
Sunscreener Lover of Some
Unseemly Forgetfulness I will call out
Your name and you will answer
Marco
                              Polo
          Olly olly oxen free

Here the trinitarian formula "in nomine patris" (in the name of the father . . .) becomes "sine nomine patris" (without the name of the father . . .), ending with a metaphor of the search for god as a children's game like Marco Polo or Hide and Seek.

The following poem, "Relocation" is an acrostic I wrote upon moving to Iowa in 2008 just after flooding had devastated much of the state and a tornado had ripped through the nearby town of Parkersburg. The poem makes an argument about how we might cut through cultural cliché to know a place more intimately and more truly.

RELOCATION

Never mind the pigs, and forget about the corn:
Observe the sky turn green with debris, the river
Restless and rising, as from sleep, where its motion is born.
To know a place, know what ancient dangers live there,
Harvest every native species of violence and grief,
Every cruel drought, every untamed coil of wind, and then
Recall that all this wildness relies on our belief:
Nature is a faith we're afraid to abandon.

Imagine the slow black halo of hawks spiraling
Out from this unlikely center: imagine some-
Where your body rooted in tallgrass, the final arrival,
Another locus of our going, a semblance to home.

Though this poem is not really about religion or atheism specifically, it expresses something very much at the heart of an atheist poetics: the fact that our lives are defined by human constructs and conventions, like the concepts of nature and wildness. These "faiths we're afraid to abandon" nevertheless influence our behavior and have real effects on the world around us and the people who inhabit it. The final poem, aptly called "The End," similarly looks to the natural world, asking that we see through the "dreams" of our own human constructs, resisting our need for "miraculous" endings.

The End

To face
Such dreams
As these:
First grief,
Deep need:
To have
The nerve
To face
These things—
As the sky
Does, or
The ocean—
Is to be
Standing,
Poised for
Lovely and
Unmiraculous
Endings.

I don't pretend that any of these poems are exemplary, but they do at least present a few modest possibilities of what an atheist poetics might look like in practice. From these specific instances I've tried to derive some general ideas that can be applied more widely.

Notes Toward an Atheist Poetics

- An atheist poetics resists, avoids, or transforms epiphany—as an idea, an experience, a literary technique. Traditionally, epiphany prompts a sudden revelation, the manifestation of some heretofore hidden truth. There's nothing wrong with revelation as such; we are all striving for some truth, idea, or insight not immediately present, or else why write poems in the first place? Rather, it's the *suddenness* of epiphany that is so troubling. Epiphany is too easy and very often imposed as a default literary device onto poems, stories, and essays.

■ An atheist poetics insists on the body as the location of human experience where truth can be found. In order to render and explore our experiences of the world, we should do so primarily through appeals to the senses and the body, not at the expense of thinking but as the unavoidable foundation of human life. Abstraction is also a valid way of knowing, of course, without which it's hard to imagine culture existing at all, much less literature. Attention to the body in an atheist poetics combats the privileging of the intellect and mind over the degraded and devalued body in western culture in general. It also keeps us honest in our literary observations.

■ An atheist poetics insists on the material world as the location of experience and meaning. The world itself is mysterious enough for our interest that if we are to discover anything at all about the universe, we're going to find it here, in the world, by which I also mean, of course, the entire cosmos, from black holes, supernovae, and dark matter, to clouds, computers, and cars. Where else could we possibly look for answers to our questions of existence?

■ An atheist poetics resists conventional spiritual or religious explanations for phenomena. Joyce Kilmer's famous (bad) poem "Trees" exemplifies this sentiment: "Poems are made by fools like me / But only God can make a tree." But there are also deeper, less obvious assumptions that can creep into art. Poets must therefore proceed with a keen skepticism concerning things that "happen for a reason." Relying on this explanation for phenomena absolves us in some larger sense of the responsibility for the world and the people who suffer in it. Another formulation of this statement is that "God works in mysterious ways." But *everything* works in mysterious ways: earthquakes, spiral galaxies, the human digestive system, quantum tunneling. We don't throw up our hands and move on when confronted with mystery. We try to figure it out, even if through metaphor and figurative language.

■ An atheist poetics insists on an openness and friendliness to science, by which I mean scientific questions, scientific findings, and scientific knowledge, not necessarily the scientific method itself. Like science, our art should shed superstitious notions of where truth is to be found and what processes we use to get there. In this regard, an atheist poetics also insists that social and environmental history have explanatory power.

- An atheist poetics insists on an awareness of the numinous and experiences of awe and wonder, but resists explaining such experiences away as religious. In these fleeting moments, there is no reason to claim to have seen through the gauzy surfaces of the material world into divine truth. Instead, this recognition is something deeply human, a realization of our animal selves, our creaturely bodies, our connection to the natural world rather than our appointment above it.

- An atheist poetics can be found in the work of non-atheists, and an atheist poetics is not always found in the work of atheist artists. An atheist poetics is not *necessarily* hostile to particular religions or religious people—though it certainly *can* be. Nor does it *necessarily* claim any fundamental or universal truth of its own. Atheism is a lack of a belief—not the presence of one. In other words, an atheist poetics is not satisfied merely with faith as a reason or explanation for phenomena. For me, an atheist poetics is actually not all that interested in the question of whether there is or isn't a god. It's more concerned with what is here now, what we can experience, and what we can learn about ourselves and the world we're inextricably a part of.

Some questions linger: how might an atheist poetics be expressed in the fantastic, the strange, the purely imagined? What is the relationship of an atheist poetics to language? What theistic assumptions are embedded in our syntax? If there is such a thing as an "atheist poetics," is there also an "agnostic poetics"? a "pantheistic poetics"? a "deistic poetics"? What are the salient differences between and among them? Does an atheist poetics offer us new ways to write poetry or think about poetry? Are there pedagogical implications to an atheist poetics?

I believe an atheist poetics is worthy of exploration and definition, if only for the lively discussions that should follow. This book represents the beginning of such a conversation. In the end, as artists, as poets, we are trying to articulate something approaching truth, even if the word "truth" is unfashionable nowadays. Shelley described himself as "a devotee at the shrine of truth," proclaiming, "Truth is *my* God." Perhaps today this truth must remain contingent, ephemeral, faint. Maybe it's complicated, too inexplicable for articulation. Nevertheless, the *necessary* challenge for atheist poets today is to create art that confronts theistic assumptions wherever they are found, that cuts through easy conventional religiosity, that affirms the material world we actually live our lives in, and that gets at what truth is to be had.

Notes

(p. 39) The sentence "Quod clara et perspicua demonstratione careat pro vero habere mens omino nequis humana" does not actually appear in Bacon's *De Augmentis* (1623), nor does it appear in its English precursor *The Advancement of Learning* (1605). The statement, however, is an apt paraphrase of Bacon.

(p. 46) The etymology section for the entry on the word "superstition" in the *Oxford English Dictionary* points out, "Classical Latin *superstes* was used with reference to a soldier standing over the prostrate body of a defeated enemy, and it has also been suggested that from this use, classical Latin *superstitiō* had the sense 'superiority,' and hence developed the senses 'prophecy' and 'sorcery.'"

(p. 49) A brief note on diction: words like "holy," "spirit," "soul," "divine," and "sacred" ring loudly of religious belief, but there's nothing inherently theistic about them at all. I believe freedom of speech, for instance, is sacred. A graduation ceremony can be holy. I can easily speak of my spirit or the soul of music without reference to a god. An atheist poetics may indeed require reappropriating so-called religious words such as these so that they no longer carry so much religiosity with them.

Martín Espada has published nearly twenty books as poet, editor, essayist, and translator. His most recent collection of poems is *Vivas to Those Who Have Failed*. Other collections of poems include *The Trouble Ball*, *The Republic of Poetry*, and *Alabanza*. Among his many honors is the Shelley Memorial Award. He is professor of English at University of Massachusetts-Amherst.

Lauren Marie Schmidt is the author of three collections of poetry: *Two Black Eyes and a Patch of Hair Missing*, *The Voodoo Doll Parade*, and *Psalms of the Dining Room*. Her poems have appeared widely, including in *North American Review*, *Alaska Quarterly Review*, and *Nimrod*. Her fourth collection, *Filthy Labors*, is forthcoming in 2017 from Northwestern University Press.

J. D. Schraffenberger is the editor of the *North American Review* and the NAR Press. He is the author of two books of poetry, *Saint Joe's Passion* and *The Waxen Poor*, and the editor, most recently, of *Manifold Nature: John Burroughs and the North American Review*. His other work has appeared in *Best Creative Nonfiction*, *RHINO*, *Brevity*, *Prairie Schooner*, *Hayden's Ferry Review*, and elsewhere.

Heid E. Erdrich is a poet, writer, and filmmaker. Her most recent book is nonfiction, *Original Local: Indigenous Foods, Stories and Recipes from the Upper Midwest*.

Andrew Sneddon is the author of *A is for Atheist: An A to Z of the Godfree Life*. He is professor of philosophy at University of Ottawa.

A Note on the Type

The Necessary Poetics of Atheism is set Adobe Garamond Pro. The typeface is based on the design of Claude Garamond (or Garamont), a printer in sixteenth-century Paris. He cut the typeface for the court of King Francis I, based on the handwriting of the king's librarian, Angelo Vergecio. Garamond's assistant, Robert Granjon, was instrumental in developing the italic type. Their collaboration on the serif face was early in Garamond's career. Both Garamond and Granjon went on to illustrious careers.

Adobe's digital version of Garamond was developed by Robert Slimbach and released in 1989. Adobe Garamond Pro followed in 2000.

Besides its versatility and elegance, the Garamond typeface is one of the most widely used digital styles because of its eco-friendliness: its slim design uses less ink than many other kindred typefaces.

Visit twelvewinters.com for author biographies, interviews, booktrailers, reviews, and purchasing information. Follow @twelvewinters and twelvewinterspress on Facebook for the latest updates.

www.ingramcontent.com/pod-product-compliance
Lightning Source LLC
Chambersburg PA
CBHW030154070426
42447CB00032B/1189